WHEN i BECAME WE

First Edition
Self and independently published in 2024
ISBN: 9798332418174

Text Copyright © Alejandra Ruíz Gómez

Illustrations Copyright © Melina Touros

The Author and Illustrator assert the moral right to be identified
as the Author and Illustrator of the work.
All rights reserved. No part of this publication may be reproduced,
stored in a retrieval system, or transmitted in any form or by any means,
electronic, mechanical, photocopying, recording or otherwise,
without the prior permission of the Author and Illustrator.

WRITTEN BY
ALEJANDRA RUIZ

ILLUSTRATED BY
MELINA TOUROS

WHEN I BECAME WE

THIS BOOK BELONGS TO

....

For all those who have a hard time thinking in terms of "us".

For my Brujita,
thank you for the inspiration.

i WAS A REGULAR i,
REGULARLY LIVING THE LIFE
OF AN i.
UNTIL ONE DAY SOMETHING
STARTED TO FEEL DIFFERENT
INSIDE...

i FEELS VERY LONELY
AND TIRED,
TIRED OF JUST BEING
FOR AND BY IT-SELF

i WANTS TO GROW.

ONE DAY i WAS GAZING AT IT-SELF IN THE MIRROR FOR A L-O-N-G TIME, WONDERING WHAT IF???

WHAT IF IT TRIED TO STRETCH IT-SELF AS FAR AS IT COULD POSSIBLY GO

SO i STRETCHED AND STRETCHED, AND STRECHED...

UNTIL IT BECAME
SO LONG THAT IT
BROKE IN HALF

THEN i LOOKS AT THE OTHER HALF AND ASKS IT-SELF WHAT IS THAT???

WHEN i TRIED TO STICK IT-SELF BACK TOGETHER, ONE HALF STARTED TO BEND IN A CURIOUS WAY

AND THEN THE OTHER HALF
TURNED ON ITS SIDE
GROWING THREE BRANCHES

NOW i WAS
NOT THAT LITTLE

NOW i WAS
NOT i ANYMORE

NOW i WAS
NOT ALONE ANYMORE

i HAD BECOME WE.

Alejandra Ruíz Gómez has been a talented writer since childhood. Born and raised in Colombia, she is now a polyglot who likes to express her ideas in the language that inspires her. She has published several audio stories for kids through digital platforms over the years.

This is her first printed book for children, and for adults whose inner child is still out there.

Melina Touros is a seasoned graphic designer. Half-Colombian and half-Greek-Cypriot, she brings an exciting mix of culture, language and experience to her work. She has an impressive record for transforming ideas into graphic and interactive design masterpieces.

Her passion to inspire kids with artistic experiences is imprinted here on her first illustrated book.

Melina y Alejandra known each other since childhood.
One of those friendships that stay intact over time,
even if a really whole lot of time has passed.
they recently re-connected via serendipity
to make this book happily happen.

Made in the USA
Middletown, DE
05 August 2024